My Favou Yorkshire Bench

compiled by Paul Griffiths

Dalesman

First published in 2020 by Dalesman Publishing
an imprint of
Country Publications Ltd
The Gatehouse, Skipton Castle
Skipton, North Yorkshire BD23 1AL

Introduction, captions & image selection © Paul Griffiths 2020
Images © contributors (as listed on page 80) 2020

ISBN 978-1-85568-389-1

Printed in China by 1010 Printing International Ltd.

Introduction

Is there anything more satisfying than a well-positioned bench just at that moment when you need one?

This book is a culmination of an idea that started more than twenty years ago with two particular benches. As a family we would make an annual trip to Hawes in Wensleydale and have fish and chips on a bench with the inscription "I lift mine eyes unto the hills" and with a marvellous view. Also, a bench on the Shawl near Leyburn is where we go to celebrate life events both sad and happy with a bottle of champagne. These benches inspired me to create My Favourite Bench.

I was challenged by my sons to stop talking and make it happen! So began my social media journey around the world. My dream is now a reality. Every day I receive images of benches from all around the world and often the reasons why they are special to the sender.

Most people have a connection with a particular bench — whether it is the view, a memory or just because they like it. I feel we all have a favourite bench somewhere … mine happens to be in glorious Yorkshire.

Paul Griffiths
https://twitter.com/MyFaveBench
http://www.myfavouritebench.com/

A sunny spring day in Ravensworth village, near Richmond.

There are great views of Ripley Lakes from this bench on the ramparts of Ripley Castle, North Yorkshire.

A frosty cloud inversion at Otley Chevin in Wharfedale.

Lazy Sunday in Saltaire on the Leeds & Liverpool Canal. Saltaire takes its name from its founder, Sir Titus Salt (1803–76), and the River Aire, which runs through the village. Salt made his fortune in the Bradford textile industry, manufacturing fine woollen fabrics.

The Walled Gardens at Beningbrough Hall, where families are encouraged to run around and play in the many different gardens that surround the hall.

The impressive ruins of Easby Abbey near Richmond. Founded in 1152, the abbey was suppressed in 1536 and within two years most of its buildings had been stripped and demolished. The ruins later became a favourite subject for artists, including the English Romantic painter J M W Turner.

One of many station benches at Pickering on the North Yorkshire Moors Railway. Pickering also hosts the ever-popular Wartime Weekend, which is held every October, and includes a full programme of Second World War and 1940s-themed entertainment and events.

The warm glow of sunset lights up the grandstand at Thirsk
Racecourse, which officially opened its doors in 1875.

The stepping stones, Lealholm village. The *Sunday Times* described Lealholm as "the prettiest village in Yorkshire". The River Esk runs through the centre of the village and these stepping stones have provided hours of fun for generations of local children.

Queen's Jubilee Bench in Egton Bridge, North York Moors National Park. This bench is perched on a small island of grass on the road to Grosmont.

The path to Roseberry Topping, in North Yorkshire. Its summit has a distinctive half-cone shape with a jagged cliff, which has led to many comparisons with the much higher Matterhorn in the Swiss-Italian Alps.

Take a seat and enjoy the darkened skies gathering over Beverley Minster, founded in the early eighth century by Saint John of Beverley, Bishop of York. The minster's beautiful west front is said to be the model for the west towers of Westminster Abbey.

This bench is situated at the south end of Coffin Pond, in the grounds of the luxurious Swinton Park Hotel near Masham.

Looking down into Cleveland from Lordstones Country Park. The area around Lordstones has been greatly affected by the mining of the jet in the area. Jet is a black gemstone which was made into jewellery and was very popular during the Victorian era.

This bench is found on the North Yorkshire Moors Rail Trail and is a welcome relief before you drop down into the village of Grosmont with its nostalgic smell of steam trains.

Millennium cairn and memorial bench,
Buttertubs Pass, Yorkshire Dales.

One of the many benches found on the North York Moors, this one overlooks Rosedale Moor.

This bench on Clay Bank in the Cleveland Hills, has breathtaking views across the moorland of North Yorkshire, and is a well-positioned resting place on one of the many walking trails.

Steam Locomotive LMS Black 5 44806 pulls into Grosmont station with its light blue benches. The train will have started its journey in Whitby and would be making its way to Pickering on the North Yorkshire Moors Railway.

44806 was retired from service by British Rail in 1968.

This bench is positioned at the south end of the bustling historic market town of Helmsley in Ryedale.

The Queen's Birthday Bench at Ravensworth, in the Holmedale
valley, Richmondshire, is to commemorate Her Majesty The Queen's
ninetieth birthday.

This bench is on one of the many coastal paths around Runswick Bay, and enjoys spectacular views across the bay and out into the North Sea.

I think we should do as we are told and "Rump Rest".
This simple bench is positioned in the dunes around Cayton Bay.

This early morning photograph has a great view of the iconic Humber Bridge, which was once the largest suspension bridge in the world and is still the largest in the United Kingdom. The bridge opened to traffic in 1981.

This unusual-looking bench is found on the Wolds Way looking towards Millington. The Yorkshire Wolds Way is a seventy-nine-mile (127km) walking route in the chalk landscape of the Yorkshire Wolds. This National Trail winds through some of the most tranquil and gentle countryside in England.

Two benches for the price of one in the unspoilt valley of Swaledale, at the northern tip of the Yorkshire Dales National Park. Swaledale is famous for its heather moors and waterfalls.

Newby Hall near Ripon is full of suntraps with benches that encourage you to sit and just enjoy the colour, sights and smells of its award-winning gardens.

Even a rainy day in Kettlewell cannot dampen the spirits of the thousands of walkers who pass through this beautiful little village every year.

This simple bench near Little Ayton has outstanding views back into Cleveland but it also has a sideways view of Roseberry Topping to the east.

This bench is on a pleasant walk near Cod Beck just outside
Osmotherley in the North York Moors.

There are many benches surrounding the twenty-foot (6m) whalebone arch on Whitby's West Cliff. The bones are there to commemorate the whaling industry that once flourished in the town during the eighteenth and early nineteenth centuries.

Sunset at Lunds Tower, near Sutton-in-Craven. The bench view is looking over towards Lothersdale with the Yorkshire Dales in the background.

This old stone-framed bench is in Fryupdale, one of the funniest place-names in Yorkshire.

Sunrise at the Cow and Calf rocks, situated above the spa town of Ilkley in Wharfedale.

Aysgarth is a small, delightful village located between Leyburn and Hawes. Aysgarth Falls are famous for featuring in the movie Robin Hood: Prince of Thieves, starring Kevin Costner.

How nice to sit on this bench at West Burton waterfall. A short walk from West Burton's pretty village green brings you to this shady spot with its small waterfall and the remains of the town mill. It is also one of the spots painted by J M W Turner on his travels in the Dales.

This bench sits in overgrown foliage outside of Nawton in Ryedale and is near the southern boundary of the North York Moors National Park.

We all love the seaside, and this bench at Bridlington is perfectly placed for us to sit back and enjoy one of its award-winning beaches.

Overlooking a stormy Rosedale. Now a peaceful, rural dale in the heart of the North York Moors National Park, in the nineteenth century Rosedale was part of industrial Yorkshire, with its ironstone mines, kilns and even a moorland railway.

When the coldness of winter has passed in Nidderdale, it's just lovely to sit on a bench surrounded by hundreds of daffodils.

On a hillside above the River Swale stands the diminutive village of Muker. This bench sits waiting for weary walkers as Muker lies on both the Pennine Way and Coast to Coast long-distance footpaths.

Storm clouds gather round this bench next to Muker Millennium
Stone Cairn above Thwaite in upper Swaledale.

A very wet bench upon Grinton Moor near Reeth, Swaledale.

A bench-eyed view of Penhill from the Shawl near Leyburn,
Wensleydale. The legend behind the name Leyburn Shawl is that
Mary Queen of Scots was imprisoned at Castle Bolton, around five
miles (8km) west of Leyburn, from July 1568 to January 1569. One
day, she managed to escape and fled through woodland, along this
escarpment, towards Leyburn, only to lose her shawl on the way —
hence the name.

This is just outside the village of Kilburn, in North Yorkshire, and has outstanding views of The White Horse. This hill figure was designed and financed by Thomas Taylor, a Victorian businessman. A native of Kilburn, he had seen the famous chalk hill figures of southern England and wanted to create something similar for his home village.

This simple bench is found in the grounds of Fountains Abbey and Studley Royal. The eighteenth-century water gardens, incorporating the ruins of one of largest Cistercian abbeys in Europe, achieved the status of a World Heritage Site 1986.

This bench situated in the grounds of St Chad's Church,
Middlesmoor, has wonderful views down Nidderdale.

Keighley Station, on the Keighley and Worth Valley Railway (KWVR). Built to serve the local mill trade in the late nineteenth century, the KWVR is just over four and a half miles (7.25km) long but still manages to pack in six stations.

Although this crescent-shaped stone bench is officially in Yorkshire, its views are looking towards industrial Teesside.

Rosedale miners' memorial stone and bench. The inscription on one side says "In the dark, working hard, loading up the wooden cart", and on the other side it reads "Work shift over, in the sun, on the hill, having fun".

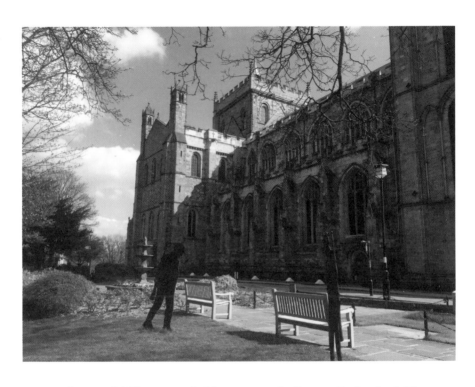

Benches and Silhouette Soldiers outside Ripon Cathedral. These dramatic six-foot (2m) metal sculptures were installed across Ripon to mark the centenary of the end of the First World War.

A plethora of benches (and a bandstand) in the gardens alongside
the Grove, Ilkley.

Beningbrough
Hall Walled
Garden.

A station bench at Bedale, on the Wensleydale Railway line which runs from Northallerton and terminates at Redmire in the heart of Wensleydale.

This very elegant bench at Fountains Abbey is rightly popular
because it overlooks Studley Royal Water Garden.

This bench in Hawes is where the seed for My Favourite Bench was planted. The inscription on the bench reads "I lift mine eyes unto the hills". Each time we visited this bench my idea would rekindle in my thoughts. I just didn't know what to do with the idea.

Springtime in Reeth. Tucked away at the junction of Arkengarthdale and Swaledale, the village of Reeth is an attractive tourist centre with a huge open green filled with benches.

Sunrise on Ilkley Moor.

A spring sunrise at Embsay Reservoir near Skipton.

Looking down dale in Rosedale.

I find nothing more delightful than sitting on one of the benches in the garden at The World of James Herriot. Sitting next to the great man himself transports me back to my childhood and the Sunday evenings spent watching All Creatures Great and Small on the TV.

The famous Yorkshire vet and author Alf Wight (James Herriot)
would call this "The best view in England". The view is from Sutton
Bank looking towards the market town of Thirsk.

A busy bench at any time of the year is this one on the beautifully named Whipperdale Bank on the road between Grinton and Leyburn in the Yorkshire Dales.

My actual favourite bench. This is where we come as a family to celebrate life events. We have been visiting this bench near Leyburn for many years. One of my favourite memories is of my young sons having a great time sledging down the snow-covered slopes.

St Mary's
Church,
Studley Royal,
near Ripon.

Which way shall we go? This bench stands near the village of Bilsdale which lies between the viewpoints of Clay Bank to the north and Newgate Bank to the south.

The start of the Cleveland Way. The Cleveland Way National Trail is a 109-mile (175 km) walking route through beautiful and ever-changing landscapes and scenery. It was officially opened on 24th May 1969 and is still very popular with walkers.

A wonderful bench view of the beach near Burniston, on the outskirts of Scarborough.

Lush greenery and flowers surround this bench in Swainby on the
edge of the North York Moors.

Steam train 41241 pulls into Damems Station on the Keighley & Worth Valley Railway.

A panoramic view over the Vale of Mowbray.

This metal version is high above the market town of Skipton,
North Yorkshire.

Summer in Harrogate's Valley Gardens, a seventeen-acre English Heritage Grade II listed garden which was developed as an attractive walk for visitors to this spa town as part of their health regime.

Nestled in the long grass, this bench at Thornwick Bay
near Flamborough has views of the North Sea crashing
into the rocks below.

The fifteenth-century Church of St Michael and All Angels stands at the western edge of Coxwold village. There has been a church here as early as the eighth century but the present building dates entirely to the period 1420-30.

Enjoying the views in Knaresborough.

Acknowledgements

Thanks to the following for submitting images:

Julie Benson

Emily Bentley

Gary Clarke

Kevin Cook

Paul Edwards

Paul Griffiths

Andrea Graham

Rose Habberley

Nick Hedges

Molly Hoggard

Nicky Johnson

Andrew Locking

David Oxtaby

Barbara Starkey

Rachael Welby

Martyn West

Mike Whorley

My Favourite Bench

My Favourite Bench exists because like-minded people share a passion for capturing images of benches, their views and their inscriptions. What started off as a simple idea many years ago is now an enjoyable escape for many people from across the globe. Whenever I mention My Favourite Bench many people just laugh, but then they think and say "My favourite bench is at...". We all have one. Share yours online at
https://twitter.com/MyFaveBench
http://www.myfavouritebench.com/